Steed Dölger
Love - The Nature of Man

Steed Dölger

LOVE
The Nature of Man

Copyright of the English version © 2016 Steed Dölger
Contact: www.steed-doelger.de

Copyright of the original German edition © 1993 Steed Dölger
Second revised edition 2004; edited 2009
Third edition 2016, ISBN 978-3-741-26643-0 (German)

This book has been translated into several languages (see p. 83).
English translation: Celine Schuman / Seymen Schuman,
December 2009

Book design: Sevira Patricia Landsberg, Troisdorf
Contact: www.sevira-consult.de

Cover: Temple of Sathya Sai Baba at Prasanthi Nilayam,
the main ashram in Puttaparthi/Southern India
Photo: private archive

All rights reserved, including those for reprinting,
reproduction and translation.

Manufactured and published by Books on Demand GmbH,
Norderstedt
ISBN 978-3-741-27339-1

*This book is dedicated
to the divine creation.
May all beings awaken
to their divine light.*

Table of Contents

Preface   *9*

Chapter:

1. *On the Essence of Love*   *11*

2. *About All That Is*   *13*

3. *On God*   *15*

4. *On Lucifer*   *17*

5. *On Creation*   *20*

6. *On the Essence of Man*   *23*

7. *On the Healing of Man*   *37*

8. On Sound
   - The Music of Love -   48

9. On Dance
   - The Play of Light -   58

10. The Play of Light
    - Life is Colorful -   62

11. On Communication
    - Cosmic Exchange -   68

12. About Your Being in the Universe   74

About Steed Dölger   81

Contact   82

Preface

My work over the decades as a spiritual teacher has shown me that we are living in a time when more and more people are opening up to their own spiritual development. More and more people are sensing that there is a soul at their core and that they want to learn to follow their own path to light. And this makes sense, since the cosmic development of man and the earth is at a point of transition, moving into the Golden Age.

In this time of transition it is necessary that people free themselves from worldly constraints and from their misunderstanding of divine love. It is time for man to live his true nature, his true Love.

This requires above all else openness and honesty. Integrating self-responsibility, meditation and prayer into the every day is what allows man's original spirituality to take place and unfold.

This book recounts mankind's most fascinating story. For the reader, may this be a loving and blessed introduction to his own spiritual world on the way to "Knowing Thyself".

Steed Dölger
Troisdorf, Germany
September 2004

Chapter 1

On the Essence of Love

Love.
Love, ever-present and never-ending.

Love is in all hearts.
Love is in every moment.
Love is the path, the goal.

Love is the light of the world.
Love is the greatest creative power.
Love is the law of the cosmos.
Love is in light and in darkness.
Love is the highest energy.

Love is the highest form.

Love is boundless.
Love is not bound by space.
Love is not bound by time.

Chapter 1 - On the Essence of Love

Love is crazy with love.

Love is a state of being.
Love is being's original form.

Love is man's reason for being.
Love is so beautiful, so pure, so powerful.

Love is in wakefulness and in dreaming.
Love is above and below.
Love is order and chaos.
Love is the wave and the fixed point.
Love is the circle and the spiral.
Love transcends it all.
Love is the purest of all energies.

Love is mankind.
Love is creation.
Love is the cosmos.
Love is the universe.
Love is everything.
Love is God.

Love, ever-present and never-ending.
Love.

Chapter 2

About All That Is

All that is, is sound.
All that is, is color.
All that is, is light.
All that is, is Love.
All that is, is being.
All that is, is God.

All that is, is true in Love.
All that is, is true and righteous.

All that is, is love, is consciousness.
All that is, stems from the one Love.

All that is, sings in the light of creation.
All that is, dances in the light of creation.
All that is, pulses in the light of creation.

Chapter 2 - About All that is

*All that is,
even the smallest cosmic dust particle,
is consciousness and all-powerful.*

*All that is,
even the smallest human cell,
is all-mighty in its consciousness.*

*All that is,
even that which doesn't believe to be of Love,
is in this way, too, a child of Love.*

Chapter 3

On God

God.

God is.

God is Love.

God is in the beginning.

God is in the end.

God is in everything.

God is that which cannot be expressed.

God is boundless.

Chapter 3 - On God

God is beyond space.

God is beyond time.

God is the transcendence of it all.

God is Love.

God is.

God.

Chapter 4

On *Lucifer*

*Lucifer,
the supposed Prince of Darkness,
prays to the power of Love.*

*Lucifer,
the misjudged one,
was always in the light.*

*Lucifer,
the bearer of light,
carries the Love in his hands.*

*Lucifer,
the Prince of Realization,
was always full of Love.*

Chapter 4 - On Lucifer

*Lucifer,
he brings the light.*

*Lucifer,
he brings the capacity for insight.*

*Lucifer,
he brings the capacity to decide,
to choose.*

*Lucifer,
his light makes it possible for man
to undertake
his own cosmic development.*

*Lucifer,
his light makes it possible for man
to return to his own light.*

*Lucifer,
he made the evolution of man possible,
so that man
would not have to live
in eternal darkness.*

Chapter 4 - On Lucifer

*But darkness still exists
on the earth,
because man holds on to it.*

*Darkness is still bound to man.
But it is in man that the darkness
will be overcome.*

*For the essence of man
is pure godly Love.*

On Creation

*Before the beginning
there was neither existence
nor non-existence
and God was not conscious
of his own being.*

*In the beginning
God recognized himself as spirit in Himself.*

*In the beginning
was the word,
and the word was
the sound,
the vibration,
the music of AUM,
and creation began.*

Chapter 5 - On Creation

*And the spirit is Love,
the infinite being.*

And the spirit is the universal soul.

And the spirit is God.

*God is the loving creation.
God is Love.*

*God created the earth
as a place for beings of Love
to consciously experience Love.*

*For all beings
are in the light
and in the Love.*

*For all beings
are light beings of Love.*

And man is one such being of Love.

He is one of God's beings of light.

*And through man's essential oneness
with God he is able to infuse the material
with light.*

*To be human means:
to be the bearer of light.*

*To be human means:
to be the bringer of light.*

*To be human means:
to transform into light.*

On the Essence of Man

*In the beginning
heaven and earth were one.*

*In the beginning
man was consciously
part of this oneness.*

*In the beginning,
man was not yet able
to differentiate.*

*Then man left the oneness
and went the way of duality.*

Chapter 6 - On the Essence of Man

*Then man left the oneness
and went the way of the self,
the path to realization.*

*Then man left the oneness
and went the way of differentiation
and cognition through the light.*

*Man
is so full of light and Love,
that he creates in himself
the possibility of separation.*

*Man
loves God so much,
he is so full of light and Love,
that he takes on the darkness
of the universe
to infuse it with his light.*

*Man
is so full of light and Love,
that he creates light
amidst the darkness.*

Chapter 6 - On the Essence of Man

*This highest form of separation,
the experience of duality,
was necessary
for the evolution
of mankind.*

*And it is man's evolution,
that makes it possible for him
in this Golden Age,
to once again overcome
this separation.*

*Man is a child of Love
in the light of creation,
but often no longer believes
to be of light and Love.*

This is the illusion that he lives.

*This is the illusion
that makes it possible for him
to be in darkness,
separated from everything
that is light.*

Chapter 6 - On the Essence of Man

*Fascinated
by the trappings
of his material nature,
man no longer sees
his true nature
in the light.*

*He no longer identifies himself
with his own godliness.*

*He no longer believes
to be of God.*

*But it is time for man
to once again open his eyes
to the light.*

*It is time for man
to become conscious again
of the light that he is.*

*It is time for man
to give up the illusion
that darkness still exists.*

Chapter 6 - On the Essence of Man

*It is time for man
to accept the notion
that he can overcome darkness
and consciously find completeness.*

*Man did not come to duality
as a result of his sins, no!*

*He came to duality,
to insight, by way of the light
because of God's grace.*

*Recognize
that it is time for you.*

*The time of darkness is over.
The light is once again
omnipresent.*

*Remember,
you are in the light.*

*Remember,
you are the light.*

Chapter 6 - On the Essence of Man

*Remember,
that as a being of light,
your essence is light and Love.*

*Remember,
that as a being of Love,
you transform darkness into light.*

*Transform
coarse energies into finer ones.
Transform
crude material into light.
Transform
with Love
and move from your darkness
into light.*

*You are light.
You are Love.*

*You are light and Love,
just as light and Love are one.*

*You are not only an object of Love,
but a subject of Love as well.*

Chapter 6 - On the Essence of Man

*You have
an extraordinary capacity
to Love.*

*Your capacity for Love,
when expressed in its highest form,
is pure Love.*

*And your duality allows you
to be conscious
of the Love.*

*Even the angels in heaven,
though beings of infinite Love,
do not have this capacity.*

*This is what distinguishes you
from other beings.*

Chapter 6 - On the Essence of Man

*You are the creator
of your Love.
You are the creator
of your self.*

*And this is made possible only through
God's grace.*

*Believe again in your light.
Believe again in your Love.
Believe again in your godliness.*

*You can do it!
Use your capacity for insight, for realization.*

*You can do it!
Use your freedom to make decisions.*

*You can do it!
Make use of your free will
and decide.*

*Come back to the light.
Come back to the universal oneness.*

Chapter 6 - On the Essence of Man

Listen inside of you
to the rejoicing
of all creation.

Listen inside of you
to the singing
in the heavens.

Listen inside of you
to the message of the light:

You are in the light.
You are the light for eternity.
You are what you are.
You are one with everything.
You are one with God.

The darkness has been overcome.
The darkness is in the light.

Open up and be ready.

Be ready
as a light-worker
to return to the light.

Chapter 6 - On the Essence of Man

*And before you return,
free yourself
from all that still binds you
to the material world.*

*Remember:
Your body is the temple
of your soul.*

*Remember:
As a being of both mind and matter
you can overcome
the darkness of material
through your light.*

*Remember:
Your mind rules over matter.
Your mind manifests itself as light.
Your mind is light in the light.*

*Remember:
Your light and your Love
overcome
the Wheel of Reincarnation.*

Chapter 6 - On the Essence of Man

Remember:
You are so full of light
that you overcome birth and death.

The message of Love is:

Man, overcome your limitations.
Man, overcome your mortality.

You are a child of the light
and all of light's energy is available to you.

You can transform your body into pure light
and once again be one with the divine light.

It's the most beautiful message there is:

You are in light.
You have arrived.
Experience your godliness.

There really is no darkness.
Darkness exists only in your imagination.

Free yourself from your
preconceptions and associations.

Chapter 6 - On the Essence of Man

*Free yourself from
your compromises and from that
which binds you.*

*You are not a slave to the material.
You are the light that makes the material
more light-rich.
You are the power of light.
You are a being of Love.
You are a being of God.*

*Love creates you.
Love steers you.
Love illuminates your way.
Love connects you.
Love characterizes you.
Love is your true being.*

*Believe in yourself and your power!
Believe in the power of your light!
Believe in the power of your Love!*

*Not a single human soul
will be lost
in God's creation.*

Chapter 6 - On the Essence of Man

*Not a single human soul
will be forgotten
in God's creation.*

*Not a single human soul
will fall the way
of eternal damnation.*

And God's glorious message is:

*Heaven and earth
will again be one
in the age of re-union,
in the golden age,
in man,
for the union takes place
inside of him.*

*This is true renewal.
This is for humankind
the true healing.*

*All souls will enter again
into the light of Love.*

Be joyful,
all men will become one again with God.
No man has ever really left God!

Be joyful,
heaven and earth will be reunited.

Be joyful
and celebrate
this cosmic union
in the garden of your soul.

Be joyful,
that is your task.

Be joyful,
that is your path, your goal.

Be joyful,
the Lord is grateful to you,
just as you are grateful to the Lord.

On the Healing of Man

Love is the greatest salvation.
Love is light in its highest form.
Love is the highest power.

All souls
are made of light
and Love.
And so is
the soul of man.

And this is why Love
is the only thing
that can truly heal.

Chapter 7 - On the Healing of Man

When man turns his back on Love.
he becomes sick.
When he returns to Love,
he is healed.

True healing always occurs
by way of Love.

True healing
means healing for man,
for humanity,
for the earth
and the cosmos.

There is great power in this healing,
for it awakens the joy and Love
that is inside you.

This healing will lead you
to your connectedness with all things.

This healing will lead you
to forgive yourself
and all other beings.

Chapter 7 - On the Healing of Man

*All beings are
brothers and sisters
of light!*

*There will be neither strife nor disunity,
for harmony and peace are in you.*

*How can you still be sad,
dejected and bitter
when you know
yourself to be of God?*

*Sadness and bitterness
only harden you,
and that is not in keeping
with your true nature.*

*Your true nature
brings harmony to all beings.
Your true nature
knows no disharmony.*

*So be happy,
for you come from happiness.*

Chapter 7 - On the Healing of Man

How can you say
you live a spiritual life
if you are not happy,
if you still doubt,
if you still feel anger inside?

You are a being of light and Love.

You can accept yourself
in this play of light.
You can lose yourself
in this play of Love.
You can be your true self
in this play of Love.

Accept yourself the way you are.

Understand
every truly spiritual life
fills you with Love.

Let your life to be filled with
joy and peace.

*And allow every being of light
to take part
in your happiness.*

Know thyself!

*Your humanness
is the highest form of being*

Know thyself!

*Recognize yourself
in all things.*

*Recognize yourself
as oneness.*

*Recognize yourself
as a being of God.*

*Recognize
your true being.*

Chapter 7 - On the Healing of Man

Recognize that you come from God.

For to come from God means:

To see everything in Love.
To accept everything in Love
and let it be the way it is.
To Love everything in Love,
as is your true nature.

This will enable you to forgive yourself.
This will enable you to forgive all souls.

To forgive means:
to accept everything the way it is.

To accept means:
To acknowledge as reality
that which you experience
in your world.

To acknowledge reality means:
self-awareness and self knowledge.

Chapter 7 - On the Healing of Man

Accept yourself completely.
Accept yourself the way you are.
Take on your darker sides.
Take them on and transform them
in your light.

To redeem your dark sides
is the most important,
most challenging,
and most wonderful task
of your life.

Engage in everything that will
help make you conscious of your soul.

This is the only way to find your calling.
This is the only way to become aware
of your purpose.
This is the only way to experience true healing:

The healing of your dis-unity
The healing of your egocentrism and vanity
The healing of your entangled humanness.

The healing of your negative attitude
towards God.

Chapter 7 - On the Healing of Man

*Do not complain
about your apparent loneliness.*

You are only alone in your imagination.

*You are also complete
when you are al(l)one.*

*You are also of God
when you are al(l)one.*

Go into the oneness of God.

*Communicate with all souls,
with the souls of men
and with the souls of plants and animals.*

*This will truly heal you,
For you will be one with the spiritual world.*

*Communicate with all that exists.
You have this capability within you.*

*You are a being of light and Love.
You need only to remind yourself of this.*

Chapter 7 - On the Healing of Man

Make contact with all that exists.
Accept your own cosmic development.

Let your humanness, your true self,
shine through again.
Let your true nature, your true form,
shine through again.
Give room to your visions again.
Give room to your laughter again.

Laughter heals you and all beings.

To laugh is to be joyful.
To laugh is to have an open heart.
To laugh is to connect and bring together
all that is.

Laugh with Love and cultivate
your sense of humor.

A sense of humor
never fails to connect.
It is something that brings together
amidst the apparent chaos
of man's self-centeredness.

Chapter 7 - On the Healing of Man

*Rejoice, laugh and share your sense
of humor!*

*For your are already in heaven,
where rejoicing and laughter
are ever-present.*

Laugh, pray, work and be happy.

*Give thanks to the creator,
who forbids you nothing.
Give thanks to the creator,
for this opportunity to be human.*

*Learn to face hardship without complaint.
Learn to face hardship and be joyful.
Learn to face hardship and praise
God's names.*

*For life is beautiful.
For life is wonderful.
For life is full of light.
For life is full of Love.
For life is worth living.*

Chapter 7 - On the Healing of Man

This is Love's message for your soul.

*There is nothing more beautiful,
nothing more valuable to you,
than living your own life.*

*Rejoice,
for the time of Love and salvation
is now!*

Chapter 8

On Sound
- The Music of Love -

*All that is,
is Love, truth and sound.*

*The universe is sound.
The world is sound.*

*Even the smallest of your cells
are made up of sound,
for light and sound are one
and the same.*

*Every frequency
has its own
individual sound.*

Chapter 8 - On Sound - The Music of Love

*And this sound can be heard,
though your ears can hear
only some of it.*

*Your heart can hear all sound,
for your heart can hear Love.*

*Your heart is the center
of Love and absolute truth.*

*With your heart you hear that
which really is,
for it is through your heart that
you connect with all that is –
with all sound.*

*When you no longer hear
creation's song of praise,
your heart is closed.*

*Then you are hardened
on the inside
and you cannot resound
the way you are meant to resound.*

Chapter 8 - On Sound - The Music of Love -

*Then you don't join
in the sound of creation.*

*If you want to hear
creation's song again
and be whole again,
then engage in music,
for music can heal you.*

*It is nature's music,
and the music of the cosmos,
that is received
by the creative beings,
the muses, and then transposed
into audible music
by gifted musicians.*

Music is an expression of Love.

*All great musicians
are so full of Love,
that their hearts overflow
with the resounding music of Love.*

The great composers are spiritual people.

Chapter 8 - On Sound - The Music of Love

They do not really compose the music.

Kissed by their muses,
they receive the music
from the heavens.

Listen
so that your heart does not harden,
so that you find your Self again
and understand
that you are brothers and sisters
of nature and of creation.

It is time
to open your heart to it again.

It is time
to bless nature
and everything in nature
that lives and loves.

Bless everything that you encounter in Love!

And you will find yourself again in the flow
of your life.

*And you will pass on
the healing
that you yourself
have received.*

*The angels
and all beings in the light,
they too listen
to the infinite sound
of the worlds.*

*Everything listens in rapture and joy
to the infinite variation of tones:
the sound of water,
the sound of a spring,
the sound of a stream,
the sound of a river,
the sound of the sea.*

*Water is also a symbol for purification.
It is light,
materialized through sound.*

*So purify yourself in this sound,
this music.*

Chapter 8 - On Sound - The Music of Love

*Water's sound touches you,
and moves you.*

*Water calms you.
It takes you back
to your very own sound,
to your own Self.*

*Even when your ties
to the material world
prevent your inner self from listening,
water's music still heals you.*

*The sound of water
opens you up inside
to the divine music,
to the cosmic sound.*

*The cosmic sound is your true being,
since you too are an expression
of Love's song.*

*So listen to water's music
to heal yourself.*

Chapter 8 - On Sound - The Music of Love

And just as water's music heals you,
you can heal the water
with your own sound.

For Love is never one-sided.

Since you are a being of light,
you can pass on your light and Love
to the springs,
streams,
rivers and seas
so that they become
more light-rich.

This is what it means to be in the flow.
This is what it means to be of light.
This is what it means to be of Love.
This is what it means to be of creation.

You can be sure,
that both water
and the creatures of the water
long for your healing Love.

Chapter 8 - On Sound - The Music of Love

*And just as you heal
all beings with your Love,
so do the sounds of nature
heal your being:
the song of the wind in the trees,
the song of a bird,
the chirping of a cricket.*

*All sounds of nature heal you.
All sound is the Love that heals you.*

*Those who think a bird's song
has little to do with music are mistaken.*

It is how birds praise creation.

*And everything that praises creation,
vibrates at the same frequency
and is an expression of the one true Love.*

*Singing is a natural form of expression
for your soul,
when it is not in its earthly form.*

Chapter 8 - On Sound - The Music of Love

The angels in heaven sing, too.

*Through your singing
you can open yourself up again
to praising creation.*

*Music is the divine vibration,
the divine frequency,
that opens you up.*

*Music is the divine vibration
that opens your heart
to the one sound of all beings.*

*Sing with Love,
for the cosmos is full of song
and full of praise for creation.*

*Open yourself up to your own song.
Give in to your own sound.
Give in to your own melody.*

Chapter 8 - On Sound - The Music of Love -

*And you will feel
your own infinite source of light.*

You will feel your capacity for Love.

*You will hear in you
God's divine music.*

On Dance
- The Play of Light -

Shiva dances
the divine dance,
the cosmic reel,
the dance of the atoms,
the dance of creation.

The entire cosmos,
all beings,
all angels,
all existence
vibrates
and
dances.

Chapter 9 - On Dance - The Play of Light

*As a being of light,
as a being of Love,
you are also a being that vibrates,
that "swings",
you are also a being that dances.*

*To vibrate, to "swing",
means to be unbound!*

To dance means to be unbound!

*Swinging and dancing
frees you from the
game of maya here on earth
and lets you experience
the play of Love inside you.*

*Love is always unbound.
Love does not let itself be bound.
Love does not let itself be clutched
nor halted.*

*To connect without being bound
is one of Love's qualities.*

Chapter 9 - On Dance - The Play of Light -

*That is the play of Love,
and in dance you experience
the acoustical expression, the sound,
of this play.*

*In dance you give in
to your own vibration
and praise creation.*

*Each and every one of your cells
vibrates and dances
in praise of creation
in the light. Each cell is light.*

*Dance is an expression of your gratitude,
for the chance to be here on earth.*

*It was not easy to come to earth
this time around,
for all too many beings would like
to incarnate as man.*

*So give thanks to the Lord
and praise him for evermore.*

Chapter 9 - On Dance - The Play of Light

*For this is the highest joy
that you can ever imagine.*

So be happy, sing and dance!

*When you dance and sing
you experience happiness,
for this is the natural form
of self-expression
that you have known
since the beginning of time.*

Dance, to free yourself

*of your bitterness,
of your hardness
of your ego-centricity.*

*Dance in the light,
for your are a light-dancer.*

*Dance,
for through your light-dance
you praise the creator
with Love and humility.*

Chapter 10

On *Light and* Color
- Life is Colorful *-*

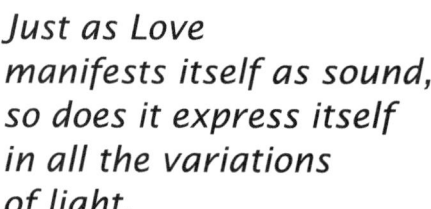

*Just as Love
manifests itself as sound,
so does it express itself
in all the variations
of light.*

*And it is these variations of light
that you perceive as colors.*

*All that is, is light.
All that is, is Love.
All that is, is color.*

Chapter 10 - On Light and Color - Life is Colorful -

You are a child of light.

You are a child of Love.

You are a child of the colors.

You are the painter of your reality,
for your life is a reflection
of your conceptions
and thoughts.

And in this mirror of your conceptions,
you realize
that life is beautiful
and full of color,
because it is part of Love's natural flow,
and
because you have the opportunity
to live it.

Heed this,
for you are
the creator
of your world.

Chapter 10 - On Light and Color - Life is Colorful -

*Heed this,
so that you do not create a world
that is colorless and dreary.*

*You alone determine
how colorful your life is.*

You decide!

*Be colorful and full of light,
and your life will be colorful
and your life will be full of light.*

*Turn away from light and color,
and you will be dark
and darkness will surround you.*

*All sadness, despair and bitterness
is just the materialized fears
from your mind
and imagination.*

*When you work with colors
you bring light into your life.*

Chapter 10 - On Light and Color - Life is Colorful -

*For the colors' light
drives away all despair
and sadness.*

*Just as nature shines
in all the colors of the spectrum,
you too can shine
in all the colors of the spectrum.*

*Bring color into your consciousness,
and your life
will be filled
with joy, levity
and the magnificent colors
of this world.*

*For you are a child of the sun.
For you are a child of light.
For you are infinitely shining bliss.*

*Every single color symbolizes
an aspect of your consciousness
and you are the sum
of all colors.*

Chapter 10 - On Light and Color - Life is Colorful -

*When you work with color,
you will come to know yourself
through the colors that you choose
and you will gain access
to your consciousness.*

*Your consciousness also expresses itself
in the color gold.*

For the Golden Age has begun.

*And in the Golden Age
gold is a natural expression of man
for he is in God
just as God is in him.*

*And he who is in gold,
cannot be in darkness.
And he who is in light,
cannot despair.*

*In light all shadows fade,
just as bitterness can only thrive
in darkness.*

Chapter 10 - On Light and Color - Life is Colorful -

*The interaction with color
is very powerful
and can help you heal.*

For you are magnificent with color.

For you are infinite.

For you are infinitely colored bliss.

Chapter 11

On Communication
- Cosmic Exchange -

*All beings
communicate with one another in light.*

*Everything is consciousness.
Everything is interconnected.
Everything flows, everything strives
to be part of the whole,
and aware of its connectedness.*

*And this is your place as man,
connected with everything that exists,
connected
with all being.*

Chapter 11 - On Communication - Cosmic Exchange -

This is your place as man,
connected and in touch
with God.

This is possible
because your soul
incarnates as man,
but still abides in heaven.

Communication
is not only
an exchange of information,
but confirmation of
your connection
to the cosmos.

This is why you are
a communicative being.

It is your nature.
Be conscious of this and seek the exchange.

Remember that you can access
all aspects of your consciousness.

Chapter 11 - On Communication - Cosmic Exchange -

*Remember that you can access
all the incarnations and earthly cycles
that you have lived through.*

*For you are, here and now,
the sum of all your
experiences and incarnations.*

*And since you have access to all that is,
let your consciousness also communicate
with your darker sides,
to infuse them with light.*

*This is how you'll learn
to communicate in Love
with yourself,
with all men,
with all beings of light.*

Remember that you can do this.

*Remember that you can
let this form of communication
back into your consciousness.*

Chapter 11 - On Communication - Cosmic Exchange -

Remember that on the soul-level,
you are connected with all that is.

Remember that you live in a time
in which man
no longer consciously communicates
with the plants
and animals of the world.

Only a few very wise souls
still know
that it is possible to communicate
with the world of plants,
animals and
even minerals.

Listen,
all sentient beings are trying
to speak with you.
There is openness from their side.

The plant world has a message for you:

Open up!

Chapter 11 - On Communication - Cosmic Exchange -

The animal world has a message for you:

Open up!

The mineral world has a message for you:

Open up!

*Open your heart and feel
your connectedness.*

*Communicate with everything
and connect with all that is.*

*Love is the language of your heart,
the language that connects everything
with everything else.*

You can do it, so believe in yourself.

*It is part of your calling, your true nature
to receive the message
of the animals, plants, minerals,
of the nature spirits,
of the devas and angels.*

Chapter 11 - On Communication - Cosmic Exchange -

*Let them into your heart
and let them share in your Love.*

*Expand your consciousness in this way,
for this is part of Love's duty.*

*Evolutionize all of creation
with the Love that is in your heart.*

*Communicate and enter into dialog
with all that is.*

True communication means:

*Realizing your own
all-encompassing divinity.*

True communication means:

*To be whole, to be one with everything,
with God.*

*Pass this along to all beings
and to all worlds.*

Chapter 12

On Your *Being* in the *Universe*

*It is time to complete what you,
as cosmic consciousness,
took on before your current incarnation.*

*Be happy.
The Kingdom of Heavens is here.*

You are free, you can achieve completion.

*Celebrate!
And give thanks.*

*Thanks to the God of Love.
Thanks to the God who has redeemed you.*

Chapter 12 - On Your Being in the Universe

Thanks,
for you have already experienced
redemption.

Thanks,
for now all other beings
will be redeemed too.

Your redemption
came through God's grace.
And the redemption of all beings
will come through your grace.

Know,
that you are responsible for all
that happens.

Know,
that the time has come
for you
to redeem all beings.

Know,
that you are on a mission of light.

Chapter 12 - On Your Being in the Universe

Know,
that you are on a mission of Love
and that this work on behalf of the world
will make you whole.

Know,
that this Deva work on behalf of creation
will make you whole.

To be human means:
to be light.

To be human means:
to be a bearer of light.

To be human means:
to be a bringer of light.

You are the messenger of light.
You are the bringer of light.

So carry your light forward.

What good is it to the world,
if you keep your light inside you?

Chapter 12 - On Your Being in the Universe

*What good is it
to the other beings of this world,
if you do not pass on the light?*

*As a bearer of light,
you must deliver the light.*

Bear and deliver the light.

Bear and deliver the light to all beings.

Illuminate the cosmos with your light.

Always remember:

*He who has ears to hear shall hear.
He who has eyes to see shall see.
He who seeks God's Kingdom
must look within himself.*

For God's Kingdom is in you.

Your body is the temple of your soul.

Chapter 12 - On Your Being in the Universe

*You experience only
the consequences of your actions.*

You experience only your reality.

*You experience only
that which you create in your inner world.*

You yourself create your world.

*You alone are responsible for all this –
nothing and no one else
can be made responsible.*

*The time for complaining and protest
is over.*

*Hell won't exist much longer.
In Love, hell is light.*

*You are already in the light,
you are light redeemed.*

You are Lucifer redeemed.

Chapter 12 - On Your Being in the Universe

So don't protest and complain.
Celebrate and rejoice.

Be joyous, exalt.
You have been freed.

You are in gold and you are the gold.
You are in light and you are the light.

All is light, just as you are in light.
All is cosmic sound, just as you are
of the cosmic sound.
All is the heavenly song of praise.

Praise forever the name of the Lord,
for everything is striving
towards completeness.

You did not come to this world
to be a missionary –
to proclaim and to proselytize,

No!

You have come to complete yourself.

Chapter 12 - On Your Being in the Universe

*So join in the singing
and be one – in harmony – with all that is.*

*Join in the singing
every chance you get.*

*Join the heavenly choir,
and sing your own song of praise.*

*Rejoice without bounds,
set no limits to your happiness.*

*Rejoice,
you are the alpha and the omega.*

*Rejoice,
you are a manifestation of divine Love.*

*Rejoice,
for the Kingdom of Heaven is here.*

*Rejoice,
for you will discover again
the Kingdom of Heaven inside you.*

OM SAI RAM

About Steed Dölger

In his tradition individuals are guided along their path to light, the golden way of the heart.

Through his light and through his Love, individuals remember their own divine origins. With "Know Thyself" as their guide, they learn that Love is their true nature.

Contact

www.steed-doelger.de

*For questions regarding the text,
please contact the translator:
celine@space-for-spirit.com*

Liebe - Die Bestimmung des Menschen
(original German version)

Translations:
(as of 2016)

Love - The Nature of Man

Amour - La destinée de l'homme

Liefde - De bestemming van de mens

Amore - Il destino dell'uomo

Miłość – przeznaczenie człowieka

Любовь – Предназначение Человека

Coming soon:

Spanish, Greek, Croatian